CROSSFIRE

A Time for Peace, War & Love

CROSSFIRE

A TIME FOR
PEACE, WAR & LOVE

John G. Krenson
CITIZEN SOLDIER MINISTER

SYNERGETIC PUBLICATIONS, INC.
HENDERSONVILLE, TN

Copyright © 2006 by John G. Krenson

All Rights Reserved. No part of this publication may be reproduced or transmitted in any form or by any means electronic or mechanical, including photocopying, recording, or any information storage and retrieval system now known or to be invented, without permission in writing from the publisher or author except by a reviewer who wished to quote brief passages in connection with a review written for inclusion in a magazine newspaper or broadcast. Any such use should be sent to the author directly once used in the publication or broadcast.

Published in the United States by
Synergetic Publications, Inc.
PO Box 1506
Hendersonville, TN 37077
615-264-3405

Books are available in quantity for promotional or premium use. For information on discounts or terms or to contact the author for speaking engagement availability or fees, please write to: John G. Krenson.

The Krenson Group
John Krenson
916 Falling Water Court
Nashville, TN 37221
(615) 545-0299
www.johnkrenson.com

First Printing: July 2006
ISBN: 0-9632248-7-5
Printed in the United States of America—Lightning Source

Book Design:
Bozeman Design
Franklin, TN
(615) 591-7857

ECCLESIASTES
Chapter 3

1. *There is an appointed time for everything, and a time for every affair under the heavens.*

2. *A time to be born, and a time to die; a time to plant, and a time to uproot the plant.*

3. *A time to kill, and a time to heal; a time to tear down, and a time to build.*

4. *A time to weep, and a time to laugh; a time to mourn, and a time to dance.*

5. *A time to scatter stones, and a time to gather them; a time to embrace, and a time to be far from embraces.*

6. *A time to seek, and a time to lose; a time to keep, and a time to cast away.*

7. *A time to rend, and a time to sew; a time to be silent, and a time to speak.*

8. ***A time to love, [and a time to hate]; a time of war, and a time of peace.***

9. *What advantage has the worker from his toil?*

10. *I have considered the task which God has appointed for men to be busied about.*

11. *He has made everything appropriate to its time, and has put the timeless into their hearts, without men's ever discovering, from beginning to end, the work which God has done.*

   New American Bible

Dedication

This work is dedicated to my wife and best friend Carrie, the center of gravity of our family. To our children Daria Grace (Dasha) and Evan Michael (Vanushka). They are God's gift to us and my gift to them is my every effort to ensure a secure world of hope for them.

This work is dedicated to my parents Ann and Gilbert Krenson. They epitomize what the unconditional love of God is all about, love that is unmerited and unearned. God knows I am blessed far more than I could ever deserve.

This work is dedicated to my friends and family who are the parish of the Cathedral of the Incarnation, the Diocese of Nashville and fellow believer friends throughout the world. Their prayers were my combat multiplier in my personal war. Their prayers strengthened my faith that the enemy within me in the end was never able to shake. They act as Christ in my life manifesting His real presence for me. I thank them as I thank God for them.

This work is also dedicated to all those who have been abandoned to brutality and oppression when we have chosen to look the other way. And to those men and women who have given their lives because they took on the mantle of responsibility to do something about it - they are our shepherds.

Finally, this work is an offering to God. God is love. Love that is strong and unafraid. Love protects its people as God as Jesus Christ gave Himself for us on His Cross and leads us to Resurrection and New Life - to true peace.

Table of Contents

	Foreword	xi
Chapter 1	Life Before 9-11	1
Chapter 2	Call to War	7
Chapter 3	In the Heart of the Beast	13
Chapter 4	How We Are Winning the War on Terror	23
Chapter 5	What Does the Average Afghan and Iraqi Think?	31
Chapter 6	Today's Soldier: Killing Machines or the Next Greatest Generation?	37
Chapter 7	What the Church Says Today; What My Experience Told Me	43
Chapter 8	What the Church in History Has Said	49
Chapter 9	Why We Must Win This War	59
Chapter 10	Q & A: Common Questions, Uncommon Answers	65
	Acknowledgements	85

FOREWORD

"This story is really about two wars." So explains the Reverend Mister John Krenson, an ordained Permanent Deacon of the Catholic Church who is also a field-grade military police officer of the Army National Guard. John, whom I am honored to know as a close friend, served a combat tour in Afghanistan in 2003-2004 where the tensions between his civilian, clerical services of sacrament and preaching and his military service of violence were brought sharply into focus.

The tension between discipleship of the Prince of Peace and the secular duties of military service has been a matter of painful, often vitriolic debate among Christians for many centuries. Many Christians deny that there really could be such a thing as "just war," that war even for apparently just reasons can have no basis in Christian faith. Others respond that that the Scriptures teach clearly that Christians are to work for justice among the nations and that sometimes aggression by nations can only, even if regretfully, be met with force; that being so, even faithful Christians may take up the sword.

I know of no one who has struggled with this issue in heart, soul or mind more seriously or with greater sensitivity than John Krenson. Were John a military chaplain, the tension he describes so eloquently would be much lessened, even vanished. But John serves his country armed with weapons of death even while he serves his Church at the altar of the body and blood of Jesus Christ and proclaiming the Gospel. To say that the tension between these two offices caused him little concern is completely to mistake John's moral character and to be blind to the real and enduring struggle of his soul.

"Duty, honor, country," is the Army officer's credo and moral compass. To read John's story is to be taken to greater, more valuable understandings of how duty can be painful and sometimes unclear, how honor can be retained even in the fog of war and how country can be ably served even by a faithful man of Christian devotion.

John's story is universal but also unique – universal because he shares in his soul the long tradition of Christian unease with the blunt instruments of politico-military policy, unique because his struggle is specifically that of a patriotic American who has pledged allegiance both to flag of country and the Kingdom of God.

Our nation and the Church are both fortunate to be served by John Krenson. This is a book for every thinking American, especially those who struggle with the tensions between Christian faith and patriotism to country, tensions nowhere more sharply defined than in wartime.

Rev. Donald Sensing
Major (ret.), U. S. Army Field Artillery
Creator and author of popular weblog
"One Hand Clapping" at www.donaldsensing.com.
Reverend Sensing is also a frequent contributor to the noted weblog
"Winds of Change" at www.windsofchange.net.

Chapter 1

LIFE BEFORE 9-11

1999 was a glorious year. It epitomized everything about the kind of man I wanted to be. I was on top of my world. The future was unusually bright, full of hope, promise and, above all, blessing.

In 1999 I was a blessed citizen. My wife, Carrie, and I had been married for six years—years of "excruciating bliss" I jokingly told her at every anniversary—and we were planning nursery room designs, preparing for the arrival of our baby, even though we had been unable to conceive the child we desperately wanted. We had met with a reproductive specialist and learned that we were excellent candidates for in vitro fertilization. We had also prayed hard, thinking of the thousands of children already in the world who had no homes or families. We had discussed adoption before and discerned that God was telling us there was a little soul already being created according to His will that He intended for us to nurture and raise. In our case this little soul—who would become our daughter, Daria Grace, the following year—just happened to exist half a world away in Russia. We considered this gift a miracle, a new beginning for our family as a new century began.

In 1999 I was a blessed businessman. One of my closest friends and I purchased a small manufacturing firm where I had worked six years earlier as general manager. The owner of the company, my former boss, offered to sell me the company rather than close its doors. She had moved on to a new career, the business was performing at only half the success rate it had when I last managed it, and no one in her family was interested in running it. I was excited about this opportunity to grasp the dream so peculiar to the American citizen—small business ownership, and I invited my friend, who had just gone through a rocky parting with his previous business partner, to join me as my partner. He was a sales guy. I was a management guy. I had a vision for the company and he had skills that complemented mine. The new century was indeed promising.

In 1999 I was a blessed soldier. Eleven years before, in 1988, I had transferred to the Tennessee Army National Guard after having served in the U.S. Army Reserve for two years. In the Reserve I had served with a Military Police prisoner of war unit in personnel and finance. I had transferred to an armor battalion so I could get out in the woods, get dirty and get with the troops. At this time, the Guard was in the midst of the transformation that President Reagan had initiated with the entire American military. The Guard was shedding its image—mostly undeserved—as a way to dodge the draft in the late 1960s and early 1970s and as an excuse to drink beer with buddies in the woods on weekends. This transformation was timely, as the Guard and Reserve would be providing nearly half of the forces that decimated Saddam Hussein's Iraqi army during 1991's Operation Desert Storm. After the war, my armor unit—not deployed in the Gulf War—was transformed into a Military Police unit as national leaders sensed the changing need in forces for a war yet to come. I served as an intelligence officer and completed two transition courses, one for intelligence officers and one for military police officers. In 1999 I was completing a four-year command of a 182-soldier Military Police Company. It had been relocated from west Tennessee to middle Tennessee in 1996 with only 22 of its soldiers, and was having great difficulty rebuilding. My battalion commander sent me there to "fix it and to build it." I took a trusted non-commissioned officer (NCO) with me to serve as the company First Sergeant and, together with the full-time unit-readiness NCO, we developed a five-year plan to build that unit and give it the foundations it would need to be deployed for a future war. (In the Army National Guard in the post-Desert Storm era, you were a fool if you didn't think that deployment was a strong possibility at some point in your career—and that was before 9-11.) In 1999 I was nearing completion of four years of that plan; the unit was scheduled to begin the first years of the next century in exercises at the National Training Center at Fort Irwin California—the Super Bowl of Army combat training. The new century was upon us.

In 1999 I was a blessed cleric. On May 14 of that year, I was ordained as a Permanent Deacon of the Catholic Church. I had completed four years of theological studies after being asked by my parish pastor to consider ordination to the clergy. In a million years, I would never have dreamed that I would serve as part of the clergy. I had always been active in my faith and, at times, outside of it as well. I had worked actively with a homeless program, served as our parish council chairman, and participated in study groups. I had developed my faith and prayer life through many struggles: a failed engagement several years prior to meeting Carrie; lost jobs; our struggle with infertility. But I never imagined I would be called by God to teach, preach and serve at the altar, to administer the sacraments of baptism and marriage, to provide comfort as a minister of funerals, and to stand not only as a public witness for God, but also as one called to lead people to God—particularly when so often in life I felt unworthy even to stand in His shadow. Yet on May 14, I stood on the altar with 24 other men, including my close friend and business partner, at the Cathedral of the Incarnation in Nashville, Tennessee. In my white robe, I stood there and felt as one with God, enveloped by the love of God as a baby enveloped by the water of the womb. I looked up at the stained glass window as the evening sun shined through, lighting my face and warming my heart. I knew that as my family watched from the pews, so, too, was my grandmother Krenson—the most devout Catholic woman I knew—looking upon me and smiling down from heaven through that window at that moment. That evening in 1999, as I stood at that altar, I felt as I had felt six years earlier when I had stood at an altar in East Lansing, Michigan to humbly and proudly marry my best friend, Carrie Lynn Sheppard.

1999 was, indeed, a glorious year ending a glorious century. Fascism had been routed, though pockets of it remained in places such as Syria and Iraq. Communism had been routed, though pockets of it remained in Cuba and North Korea. The world spoke of a "peace dividend," though militants were at work hijacking a religion in places such as Saudi Arabia, Iran, Pakistan, and Afghanistan. The world failed to listen when a terrorist mastermind named Osama Bin Laden declared war on it, and particularly upon the United States, in 1996. We were at war but we didn't know it. The struggle still lay ahead.

1999 was a glorious year. Fatherhood was within my grasp. The American dream of small business ownership would be realized. A unit of military police was successfully being built and coming together. And I was closer to God than ever, preparing to share the comfort, love, and hope of Christ in the most humble of ways. I was at the greatest moment of peace and hope in my life.

I had no idea that the greatest struggles of my life as a citizen, soldier, and minister still lay ahead.

When I look back on 1999, now many years in my past, I look at it through a different prism, a prism shaped by the struggles of the intervening years, struggles that I have lived through and will live with forever. And while I still live my life as I had in 1999—with hope, promise and blessing—it is a life quite different from what I could have ever imagined it to be in 1999.

In 1999 everything was possible. The sense of peace within myself and within the world was palpable. Things weren't perfect. I knew that. The world knew that. I knew fatherhood and business would bring challenges. I knew service in the Guard could mean service overseas at some point. The world knew that the "New World Order" and "Pax Americana" would be challenged. But it seems to me that I—we—had a naive optimism at the time. A bright blue Tuesday morning in September 2001 would change all of that for all of us.

Chapter 2

CALL TO WAR

September 11, 2001, was a snapshot day; everyone remembers where they were on that fateful morning. I was at the dentist's office, having finished my check-up and scheduling my next appointment. Someone mentioned having heard on the radio that a plane had crashed into the World Trade Center. As people looked quizzically about, I remember thinking it must have been some fool who crashed a private plane into the building in a poorly advised stunt gone tragic. I didn't think much more about it as I walked out to my car, got in, put a CD in the stereo, and drove the twenty minutes to work. It was when I walked into our office conference room, first seeing people in tears and then looking at the television, that I finally realized our shared horror.

March 19, 2003, unlike September 11, is not a snapshot day for most people. For me it was. On that day I sat with my wife in a hotel room on Moscow's Red Square after we had just received custody of our son, Evan Michael, our second adopted Russian child. On Russian television, we watched American troops launch the campaign into Iraq. Three weeks later, after returning home with Evan, I would receive my mobilization alert for Operation Enduring Freedom in Afghanistan.

September 11, 2003, is not a snapshot day for most people. For me it was. On that day, I found myself just down the street from the U.S. Embassy in Kabul, Afghanistan, right in the heart of what had been Taliban country, the place where the attack just two years earlier was born. On that night, after having been in the country for only a few weeks, our unit would experience our first official greeting from the enemy—indirect rocket fire in Kabul.

My story is about two conflicts.

One conflict—the one fought with weapons on the battlefields of Afghanistan—is pretty obvious. The other conflict, however, is one I have fought all of my adult life— the tension between being a Christian man and being a military man, a tension between my humanity and my search for divinity.

I've been associated with the military in some capacity all of my adult life. When I arrived at Marquette University in Milwaukee as an eighteen-year-old freshman, the first building I entered after unpacking my dorm room was the ROTC building. The tension arose fairly early for me. As an ROTC cadet, I would lay in my bunk at night, questioning whether a good Catholic could or should also want to be a good military officer. It would often keep me awake, as I sought resolution, which was hard to find. I was caught in the crossfire of a seemingly contradictory question: could the ideal—being a good Catholic and a good officer— become real?

I continued in the program—finding that the tension returned with decreasing frequency—and graduated from Marquette and ROTC in 1986, accepting a commission into the U.S. Army Reserve, and, later, transferring into the Tennessee Army National Guard. I had never really resolved the tension; it simply didn't manifest itself anymore. I was following my conscience. I believed that it was right.

But then, in 1995, things got interesting, when I was called to the Catholic Diaconate as a Permanent Deacon, a degree of Holy Orders in the Catholic Church - ordained ministry. My soul searching returned and intensified. Now, my struggle was no longer private, no longer between being merely a Christian man and a military man. I was now being called to serve very publicly as a Christian man serving as a witness for the church, while being also a military man. And, were I to continue in the Guard, I would not continue as a chaplain; I would continue to be an officer, a soldier - a potential combatant.

I had to think about how, on one weekend, I could don my minister's robe and preach about peace from the pulpit, and on the next weekend, don my officer's uniform and train with my soldiers to fight and kill our enemy. I could think about it, but I didn't have to resolve it—at least not yet. We were living in the era of the peace dividend, when the philosopher Francis Fukuyama had said that history was over with the fall of communism—that we were on our way to free markets and free societies.

I postponed that resolution during those years of apparent peace, because I thought I was following my conscience. Perhaps it was merely procrastination—or it was denial or simply cowardice—that kept me from addressing the rising tension between my two roles.

September 11 changed all that. I knew on that day that I would eventually be deployed for war. It might have been for two weeks, two months, or two years, but it was going to happen. My focus would have to shift; I didn't have time to resolve anything, because I had to prepare for war, and to prepare my family for my absence. I had to prepare for that absence with the hope that it would be temporary, but the possibility that it could be permanent.

But questions lingered in the back of my mind, "How can I justly go to war?" "What is peace?" "How just is it when we go to war?" "What is worth fighting for, dying for, killing for?"

And I asked the question whose answers disturbed me most, the question that I didn't hear from anywhere else, "How just is it when we don't go to war?"

With these questions in mind, caught in the crossfire again, I went to Afghanistan.

Chapter 3

IN THE HEART OF THE BEAST

I want to help you paint a picture of Afghanistan in the late 1990s. I want you to imagine you are a citizen in Afghanistan during the reign of the Taliban. Specifically, I want you to imagine you are a young woman in Afghanistan.

You wear a garment covering you from head to toe, every inch of your body. You wear this garment, this burka, anytime you walk out the door of your home, which is probably a mud hut or, if you are fortunate, a small compound, a little piece of property with a wall around it.

Of course walking out the door is not as free as it seems. You certainly can't walk out the door alone. Or with your sisters, or your girlfriends, or even with your mother. You could only walk out the door and into the public with a male relative—your father, your brother, your uncle, your cousin.

The physical act of seeing in this world is a difficult proposition. As you walk about wearing your burka in the company of your male relative, you see the world only through a screen in your burka. (Open the fingers of each hand, allowing only a little gap to appear between them. Cross the fingers of each hand over each other to form a series of X's. Now hold this up to your eyes and look at the world; you'll see it as an Afghan woman. I know this; I've worn a burka. My fellow soldiers and I each tried on burkas. We chuckled at first when we saw one another wearing these garments. Our chuckles died when we realized that this was the view of the world some people had.)

So now you are out in public, in the company of a male relative, and you have gone to the market, peering at goods with compromised vision. For whatever reason—loose stitching, a burst of wind—the screen covering your face has flown open, exposing your face for all to see. Within minutes—it seems like only seconds—the religious police, who lurk about everywhere, respond. Their response is swift and it is harsh: they throw acid in your face, scarring your face permanently. That will teach you never to have the vanity to show your face in public again.

This was the punishment. This was the norm.

Weeks later, after you have "recovered," you go back to market with your male relative, this time with your burka screen incredibly secured. No acid this time. You reach for a piece of fruit with your gloved hand. But the hem on your glove has sagged, and, as you reach for the fruit, an inch of your bare wrist flashes beneath the sleeve of your burka. In an instant they're upon you again, this time beating you across the back with a rod. The religious police will not tolerate such indecent exposure; it would tempt the males around you.

This was the punishment. This was the norm.

Now imagine that you are an older woman in Afghanistan, perhaps in your early fifties. In the 1970s and 1980s, before and even during the times of Soviet occupation, you had been a professional—a doctor, a lawyer, a teacher. No longer. Now, in the late '90s, the Taliban are in power. You have most likely lost your husband, perhaps in the Afghanistan Civil War. You have probably lost a significant number of male relatives to the "civil" war with the Taliban, or, perhaps, to the Soviet invasion.

You are alone, and you are essentially a prisoner in your home, because you have few male relatives left to escort you in public. And you have been this way for six years. One day, in December 2001, you learn that American troops have entered your country, liberating your town. You can now walk free. And you can leave the burka at home if you choose. You venture out from your mud hut, your compound, and you walk maybe twenty-five yards, fifty yards, and you realize that your legs don't work as they used to six years ago. But how could you expect them to work as they once had, back when you were able to walk where you wished, when you wished? You did not notice the atrophy that had beset your muscles during walks that were limited only to the boundary of your tiny home. Six years of confinement will do that. Though a bullet has never grazed you, a mortar round has never shaken you, you are one of the war's many wounded. You have lost much of the use of your legs.

Though men were in slightly less perilous straits than women during this time, they were no freer, either. If you were a man, you were required to grow a beard, and you were discouraged from cutting your hair. If you shaved or, worse, were physically unable to grow a beard, you were beaten, perhaps jailed. You couldn't listen to any music or watch television; to do so would be "idolatrous." You could not keep records of your property, your genealogy, your birth certificate. All records, all archives were "idolatrous."

You couldn't fly your kite, the Afghan national pastime. As Americans love football and basketball and baseball, Afghan men love their kites. Before these dark times, Afghans built beautiful kites and competed with each other in kite fights that took place in the air above villages and the cities. But no longer. During the six years of the Taliban reign, kites were "idolatrous."

Some Americans may think about this and think, "That's awful. What a horrible existence for these people." At the same time, another thought bubbles up, "But what does that have to do with me?"

To answer that question, I ask you to imagine yourself in another place. This time you are an American. You took the subway to work this morning, emerging from the station to a sky so blue it begged to be remembered. You walked to your workplace and rode the elevator to your office near the top of the South Tower of the World Trade Center. You have been steadily at work for nearly an hour, when you hear a loud boom outside. You run to the window to see what happened. Seventeen minutes later, the same thing will happen to your building. Your entire life will come down to two choices, one decision: do I jump to my death or do I burn to death?

This is how the situation in Afghanistan affected you. The sanctuary provided by a society like the Taliban in Afghanistan made it possible for Osama Bin Laden's evil to reach out and touch all of those innocents in the World Trade Center, the Pentagon and in a Pennsylvanian field on that dreadful day.

September 11, 2001 was not the first battle in the War on Terror. This was not the first time we had seen what Al-Qaeda could do. This war had been fought for many years before.

We know that Al-Qaeda was behind the first bombing of the World Trade Center in 1993. We know that Al-Qaeda and Bin Laden were behind the bombing of the Khobar Towers in Saudi Arabia, killing Americans there. We know that they were in Bosnia, in Chechnya, in the Philippines. We know that Al-Qaeda and Bin Laden were behind the bombings of U.S. embassies in Kenya and Tanzania, in 1998, as two hundred innocent and mostly local nationals were killed in those attacks. We know that, in 1998, Osama Bin Laden publicly and directly called for the death of all Americans and all Jews and their children. We know Al-Qaeda was behind the bombing of the U.S.S. Cole in 2000, as it made a port call in Yemen. We know about 2001: the World Trade Center and the Pentagon. United Flight 93 was the first battlefield that saw Americans fight back.

Al-Qaeda has made no attempt to conceal its ambitious goals: to develop weapons of mass destruction; to destroy Israel; to intimidate Europe; to assault the American people and manipulate them into isolation; to establish Islamic regimes in the Islamic world. We know their desires.

We also know their fears. I learned what they are up close on a Saturday in Panjwai, Afghanistan.

Saturdays in Afghanistan were often quiet days, because they followed the quiet Muslim holy day of Friday. This Saturday in February was no different. The day shift had been on duty for about three hours. We had gotten through the initial flurry of work that took place every morning. Having received, processed and sent out our reports, we now sat in our Operations Center with that breath of fresh air often reserved to a Saturday following our "morning storm." It was nice to just sit and relax. The air hung still with dust—even inside. The TV hummed with the Armed Forces Network on the screen as we monitored the news to see if it jibed with what we knew was happening. One soldier took these spare moments to check his email; an officer took advantage of the time to sit with his legs stretched out while he could. Other soldiers occasionally dropped in to grab something for the commander next door or to pass on a message. A couple of us intelligence types spent the time completing our weekly provincial threat activity analysis, surfing through reports on our laptops and making judgments as we tallied the week's activity in each of the then 32 Afghan provinces.

Then, like lightning, the Ring Road Project Liaison Officer burst into our Ops Center, slamming the wood door wide open and pounding through like a fullback. A Ring Road project helicopter was down and taking hostile fire just southwest of Kandahar. The liaison officer was in radio contact with his base of operations, which was in contact with one of the chopper's passengers currently under fire.

(The Ring Road project was the major civilian endeavor to improve the road between Kabul and the major cities of Kandahar to the south and Herat to the west. The project would decrease travel time between the major cities from days to hours and improve the flow of commerce, the delivery of health care, and access to education. This road would transform the quality of life for Afghans. The team aboard the chopper was a group of civilian engineers and planners who were inspecting a school construction project and setting up health clinics just west of Kandahar in the district of Panjwai. Now, instead of inspecting schools and building health clinics, they were fighting for their lives as bullets whizzed by their heads.)

The initial reporting indicated the chopper was shot down, three were killed, one was seriously wounded, and the Afghan interpreter had survived. He was talking on the radio while fighting off enemy fire upon the downed aircraft. With one hand he held a radio to his face while with the other hand bouncing like a jackhammer he fired rounds and screamed in a language that wasn't his own. He knew that lives, including his own, depended on every English syllable he spoke and every bullet he sent toward his enemy. Those of us in the Ops Center bolted into action, our chairs rolling out from under us. We manned map boards to plot positions, and sprang to grab communications gear to coordinate with the Combined Joint Task Force 180 (CJTF-180) operations center for a quick reaction force (QRF) and MEDEVAC for the wounded. In the chaos our minds and bodies moved with purpose. Everyone stayed cool, despite the rising pressure. We determined the crash site location and maintained radio contact with both the Ring Road base ops and CJTF-180. A B-1 bomber was dispatched to provide a show of force, and it brought the enemy firing to an end. The B-1 that had brought joy and relief to one Afghan fighting for improving that road also brought fear and death to those who were satisfied with dirt roads that led to ignorance and destitution. A ground QRF made it to the scene within an hour, and, within minutes, a MEDEVAC bird was on the scene to assist the wounded.

We learned later that the chopper was shot down as it was hovering during takeoff, killing the pilot. Among the wounded was a young woman shot in the abdomen and another man with four bullet holes in him. The Afghan interpreter, who accompanied the group, unloaded six to seven magazines of ammunition into the enemy attackers while maintaining radio contact with base ops as he defended himself and the western "infidels" from the Taliban.

Two days later, the civilian Security Coordinator for the Ring Road project personally came to Kabul and to our liaison team to thank all of us in the Ops Center who took part in coordinating the operation. The Security Coordinator, a retired Marine Lieutenant Colonel, gave high praise for our efforts, telling us that our team saved lives that day. He couldn't believe how quickly the QRF and MEDEVAC were coordinated and executed. Weeks later each of us also received a special letter of thanks from the theater headquarters Combined Forces Command - Afghanistan Commanding General.

Later that night I sat in my corner of private space at the safe house and processed the events of that day. The people we helped save that day were in Afghanistan to improve the lives of the local citizens. They were not combatants. They were road builders, school constructors and health clinic specialists. They were husbands and fathers and even a daughter. They were light skinned and dark skinned. Due to events beyond their control they were in a helicopter that day— an American, an Australian, a "Brit" and two Afghans suspended for a few moments in time over the earth they sought to improve. They were there to help build roads - roads of pavement, roads of literacy, roads of healthcare - that would enable the creation of jobs and the flow of commerce— roads that would one day carry Afghans to work, would carry brightly colored trucks loaded with goods, such as medicine and food for Afghans. Roads of literacy and healthcare that would give people opportunity and power to control their lives. These "roads" would have signs that Afghans could read. These "roads" would be the means to carry voters figuratively and literally to polls and newly elected parliamentarians to places of decision-making and influence in Kabul. These "roads" would lead to true security and freedom.

I began to realize that the Taliban and Al-Qaeda feared these unarmed "road builders" as much (if not more) than they feared our battle-hardened military forces. They feared anyone who could produce lasting change. They feared anyone who brought the lasting change of healthcare and literacy. They feared anyone who could give the average Afghan the opportunity to see through the hopelessness and the brutality of the Taliban. And the Taliban and Al-Qaeda understood all too well that that sort of lasting change meant the end of their stranglehold on power.

This event helped me to see the true nature of the enemy we were facing. It was a demonstration to me that this war wasn't just about territory—the security of ours or the control of theirs—but it was about the kind of world that was going to be shaped during the next century. It was about ignorance versus literacy, oppression versus hope, slavery versus freedom. It was about looking at the world through the screen of a burka or through an open window. This realization held spiritual and ministerial implications as it did military and political ones. It held moral implications as significant as the military action we took— or didn't take.

Chapter 4

HOW WE ARE WINNING THE WAR ON TERROR

We have responded. And the "we" is more inclusive than our news coverage would suggest. Muslims are fighting with us. Iraqis and Afghans. Allies from Saudi Arabia, Egypt, the United Arab Emirates, Qatar and Kuwait. Pakistanis are fighting with us. Kyrgyzstanis are fighting with us. The average Arab has not risen up in the way that Bin Laden anticipated. To the contrary, empowered by an alternative—the strength of this multinational force—they have risen up against Al-Qaeda.

By fighting this War on Terror, the U.S. and its allies are thwarting this plan, preventing this brutality and oppression from establishing a foothold throughout the Middle East and in Central Asia.

Let me give you an example of how this has been manifested. When I was in Afghanistan in December 2003,

I had the great privilege of being present in Kabul during the Loya Jirga, the constitutional assembly, when Afghans voted on their first constitution by sending forth delegates to Kabul to participate in this historic assembly. These delegates came from all across the country and from every ethnic group in Afghanistan. And yes, the delegates included women.

On the first day of these proceedings, as delegates took their turns making initial comments, a young woman, Malalai Joya—all of 26 years old—from Farah, a province in the southwest corner of Afghanistan, stood in Kabul at the Loya Jirga. Not only did she stand there, which itself was noteworthy, she took control of the floor. First she thanked the elder Afghan statesmen of this assembly - the warlords - for what they had done to drive out the Soviets and the Communists. But then she wagged her finger. She accused them of greed, of pride, of being anti-women, of fighting each other in the 1990s, creating the vacuum that the Taliban were only too eager to fill. She warned them against further corruption, calling upon them to seize this opportunity and establish a future for Afghanistan.

This young woman showed her face. She raised her voice. How dare she? How dare she?

The Afghan National Army was present that day at the Loya Jirga to provide security. As she spoke, the Afghan National Army soldiers rose and surrounded her. Some of the delegates walked forward, challenging her. Then the leader of the assembly stepped up and took command of the stage and defended her right to speak out. Many of us thought he was shrewd to avoid a confrontation, which would show the American press even a flicker of corruption in this process. He let her speak, provided her security.

At the same time, however, we feared that she would

likely be dead within a few months, dragged from her home in Farah in the middle of the night and executed for having the audacity to act so... free.

But as of this publication, this young woman still holds the seat in Parliament to which she was elected on September 18, 2005, and she continues to criticize and hold the new government accountable even under the continuous threat of death. And she, this woman who took the oath of office in Kabul in January 2006, is a patriot. Those who voted for her through the electoral process are patriots. And they are all brave. This is not only amazing; it is miraculous.

How miraculous? Let's go back in time—fall 2003—to Afghanistan once again, this time imagining yourself as a teenager. You live in a small Afghan village in the rugged mountains that form the Afghanistan-Pakistan border.

In your village there's been a lot of talk about the coming of democracy. It's been talked about now for nearly two years. You've been hearing that some people will be coming to talk to your village about choosing leaders, about voting. Today these people, these strangers, walk into your village. You've never seen people like this before: a white man and white woman; a black man and a black woman; an Asian man; a Hispanic woman. They begin talking to your parents about this democracy. Your parents talk back and forth with these strangers, these foreigners. Then your parents take a card and sign their names. They are now registered to vote.

The whole family is excited—this is a historic day. Your parents take this card into your home and they secure it in a spot of honor, saving it and protecting it for that day months from now when they will be able to vote. It is difficult to go to sleep that night, because everyone is so excited. But the night goes on and people eventually fall asleep.

In the middle of the night, you bolt awake. The door to your hut is smashed in. In the shadows you see two men, their heads covered with hoods. They find your parents, grab them and drag them outside. Two more hoods enter your home. They knock over tables. They knock over your cupboard. All the while they are screaming and yelling. One shrieks as he holds aloft a tiny object—your parents' voting card. He charges out the door into the night air outside where your parents are face down in the dirt.

You timidly slink out your door behind the hoods as they file out of your home. The man with the card kneels down next to your father—grabbing him by the scruff of the neck, pulling his face out of the dirt. He shoves the card in front of his face screaming at him. He slams your father's face back into the dirt, right next to your mother face buried in the dirt. Two of these hooded monsters step up with their AK-47's. They put the cold steel of those circled muzzles against the temple of your parents' heads and they blow their brains out, right in front of you. Then they flee across the border, back to Pakistan.

Your parents are a message to the village down the road: when the UN voting registration team comes to your village, you should consider the consequences of registering.

The Afghans didn't back down; nearly all that were eligible to vote—ten million citizens—registered. This was occurring as I served in Afghanistan. But they went beyond registering; in their first presidential election, 70 percent of eligible voters cast their ballots... and nearly half of them were women. (The very first voter in the presidential election was a nineteen-year-old girl.) More than 50 percent of the population turned out again to vote for Parliament a year later, which included the brave young woman from Farah.

That is democracy.

I have spoken many times in many places since returning from Afghanistan. As I spoke on a college campus in Ohio, my hosts told me with great pride the feat they had accomplished in the 2004 elections: increasing voter turnout to between 35 and 40 percent. And I smiled as I reminded them that that was barely half of the voter turnout in Afghanistan, and just more than half of the voter turnout in Iraq, where 60 to 70 percent have voted three times in elections in Iraq. And in both countries, the people voted under the threat of death. The simple threat of rain can keep many American voters at home on Election Day. But even under threat of death, Afghans and Iraqis flock to the polls.

The Afghanistan economy is experiencing 20 to 30 percent growth per year. A five-star hotel, the Serena, has been built in Kabul. The new Kabul City Center Mall rivals any mall in any American city. All of these bring hundreds of new jobs to Kabul. While that may not sound like much, it is because of these examples that foreigners will come to Afghanistan, bringing their investments and the potential of thousands of jobs.

Girls are going to school. Women are opening businesses. Women are free to walk about—many wear burkas, but it is often now by their choice. Kites fill the skies in villages and the cities in Afghanistan. Music fills the air at markets.

While Afghanistan still has a long way to go and the threat to this progress still exists, we don't hear about these amazing successes.

Let me give you an example of a success that has occurred, the kind that we would expect to hear on the news, the kind of success that will build long-term security and hope both for Afghanistan and our nation.

In the central highlands of Afghanistan is Bamiyan Province. Many people in the West remember, in the late 1990s, when the Taliban blew apart two ancient Buddhist statues in Afghanistan. It happened in Bamiyan Province, in one of the most mountainous—and most remote—regions of the world. The world heard, and was appalled by, the news of the destruction of the two Buddhist statues. The world did not hear, however, that at the very same time in the very same province, the Taliban had massacred ten thousand of their fellow Muslims, because they were Hazaras, an ethnic minority group who are also Shiites. The stories the press chose to emphasize about this province—a place where women had been denied any rights, a place where thousands were slaughtered by their own countrymen—were about the destruction of two statues.

In this remote province we have built a university. It is open to women. It serves a persecuted ethnic minority among Muslims. The U.S. flew the entire foreign press pool from Kabul to this province for a ribbon cutting with the Afghan Minister of Education to celebrate this incredible long-term opportunity for success. Fewer than a dozen press reports were filed across the world, and they were in the Hindustan Times, the Xinhua Press in China, and one tiny blurb in the West, that barely rated a mention in Western papers. Where are the stories?

We hear about improvised explosive devices that wound or kill 15, 30 or 50 Iraqis—the body count seems to be the thing. We don't hear what happens two hours later, when Iraqis line up, often at double the number, to serve their country, to risk their lives to do what they know it takes to bring peace and security and hope to their country.

We don't hear about the nine other IEDs that have been

pointed out to U.S. and coalition troops by the Iraqi locals. We don't get the attention on a regular basis of the success of the elections in Iraq.

Chapter 5

WHAT DOES THE AVERAGE AFGHAN AND IRAQI THINK?

Early in my tour of duty in Afghanistan, we stayed in a safe house run by Afghans. They provided our security. They served our meals. They ran errands for us. One of those who took care of us was a young man in his twenties. We asked him what he thought about the American presence in Afghanistan. (Of course we figured he would answer pretty positively, since we were paying him his salary.)

His face lit up and his eyes grew wide: "It is a miracle what has happened in the last two years since you threw out the Taliban." He told us that Afghanistan had seen more change in two years than it had in the previous two hundred years. Then his face grew tight, and his eyes narrowed, and he asked, "Major Krenson, I ask you, how long will you stay? Because they know who we are and they know where we live." I knew the sincerity of his answer to my question when he posed his own.

The gravity hit me that these brave Afghans who were making a living now by working for the U.S., were also risking their lives. If we left, they would surely be executed. Many of these young men who had already been beaten or jailed (or both) by the Taliban, could lose their lives.

Statistics tell us what Afghans and Iraqis think of U.S. forces in their country. At the time that U.S. troops entered Kabul in 2001, the city's population was just under one million. Before it withered under the tight grip of the Taliban, Kabul had been a thriving city of nearly 2 million residents. By the time my unit arrived in Kabul in 2003, the population had just crept back over a million. And after I returned home, the population continued to grow, to between three million and four million. Every month, thousands are leaving refugee camps in Pakistan and returning to Afghanistan. Afghan expatriates who had fled the Soviets and fled the Taliban to Western Europe and North America are returning to Afghanistan.

Follow the feet of Afghans from refugee camps and safe havens across the world. Follow their feet as they go back to Afghanistan and that will tell us what they think of what is happening in their country. People go where hope is.

The same thing applies to Iraq. One surprising miscalculation in the war in Iraq was the expectation that hundreds of thousands of Iraqis would flee as we entered their country, establishing refugee camps in neighboring countries while the war raged on. But where are the massive refugee camps holding Iraqis in Northern Saudi Arabia? In Jordan? In Syria? In the south of Turkey?

They don't exist. Because even though Iraqis have had

wide open borders for the first time in decades, most are staying in their villages and staying in their cities, despite having the opportunity to flee. The most significant refugee Iraqi population is a large group of Baathists, former members of Saddam Hussein's deposed regime; they have found hope in Syria. But the everyday Iraqi stays, because they find hope at home.

In Kabul I had the great fortune to visit an orphanage during my tour. We brought a truckload of humanitarian supplies, stuffed animals, canned goods and other necessities, things that had been shipped to us by family and friends from home in America. We dropped them off, expecting to exchange pleasantries with the director of the orphanage and be on the road again in twenty minutes. We were there for two hours. As we walked out of the director's office we looked down a hallway. From doors of the classrooms that lined the hallway, we would see an adult head poking out about five to six feet off the floor. And just a couple of feet below that head we'd see two or three little heads poking out, all of them looking for the Americans.

They knew who we were. They knew that we were soldiers. We wore our desert camouflage uniforms. Our young soldiers had their M16 rifles slung across their backs; we officers had our pistols on our hips. Military uniforms can often invoke fear, but in our uniforms, the people in that orphanage saw hope.

Despite being there two hours, we did not visit every classroom or every student or every teacher. A few minutes from that two hours I'll never forget. We were in a classroom of girls about ten to twelve years of age with their teacher. My boss, Lieutenant Colonel Jewell Fields, asked these young girls, through our Afghan interpreter, what they wanted to be when they grew up. And they responded, "I want to be a doctor." "A teacher." "An engineer." "A lawyer." And then one girl said, "I will be president of Afghanistan." And we all laughed. Not at her, but with her. We knew that, less than three years earlier, she would never have been able to dream this dream.

Just three years earlier, her teacher would have been beaten, jailed, or even executed for "infecting" the minds of young girls with such dreams. These dreams were possible because they were now dreamt by free people, people who supported a woman's candidacy for president - Massouda Jalal - in the presidential elections, and had voted for her in such numbers that she had come in sixth place in a field of seventeen candidates. These are good, amazing things, these changes happening in Afghanistan and in Iraq.

I reflect upon the early, slow development of democracy in our own country. Our own fight for independence, which began in 1775, would see a year pass before we could even agree upon a declaration of what that independence meant. It would be another year before we would submit the Articles of Confederation that would govern our colonies and their quest for independence. Four more years would pass until those articles would be ratified finally. Nine more years would pass after that, until 1790, when we would agree upon a Constitution, because of the shortcomings of the Articles of Confederation.

Fifteen years. From 1775, when we began our quest for independence, to 1790, when we finally settled on our Constitution—if, indeed, you can use the word "settled" to define a document that has been amended 27 times since its birth. (Two of those amendments, the 15th, which removed race as a bar from voting, and the 19th, which gave women the right to vote, were ratified 80 years and 130 years, respectively, after the Constitution was ratified. The amendments also saw a Civil War pass between them. The story has been much the same for much of the western world—with the most extreme example being Switzerland, which didn't give women the right to vote until 1971.) Afghanistan and Iraq have moved at a pace far more rapid than the Western models that they have adopted. (Iraq gave women the right to vote before it even adopted a constitution.)

Change takes time—and time itself is always changing. But we're already seeing an incredible ripple effect beyond the initial splashes of democracy in Afghanistan and Iraq. We are now seeing legitimate elections in several countries in that region, mostly at the local level, including Saudi Arabia and Kuwait, the latter of which, in 2006, saw women run for office (and women able to vote for them). We have seen the first meaningful presidential elections in Egypt. We have seen elections in Qatar, Lebanon, and Palestine—all three elections permitting female voters and female candidates.

These are the fruits of victory that have grown from the seeds of war.

Chapter 6

TODAY'S SOLDIER: KILLING MACHINES OR THE NEXT GREATEST GENERATION?

Who has sown these seeds? The farmers, for the most part, have been selfless and brave (and mostly young) American military men and women. Their stories are worth hearing, because they are timeless and because they can remind us of the sacrifices made by those upon whose shoulders rests our own democracy…

…like the 20 year-old medic from the Tennessee Army National Guard who rushed into a United Nations building and a Red Cross building that were crumbling from bombings. He ran in, without regard for his own life, not to rescue U.S. soldiers, but to rescue the people working there—most of them Iraqis. He ran in and out of these buildings carrying out the wounded, with the threat of collapse imminent.

...like the story of a Marine lieutenant on "the tip of the spear," who, within the first hours of the initial assault into Iraq, had his young body strafed with bullets from AK-47 fire and shrapnel from rocket-propelled grenades. He left that battlefield crying—not from his wounds, but because he did not want to leave his fellow Marines behind. He returned to the States to recuperate (it wasn't his choice), and he received one Purple Heart for his multiple life-threatening injuries. But he came back and fought his way back to the front. I had the privilege to serve alongside him in Afghanistan. Deep in the war zone, he continued to try to find ways to get back to the front lines, whether in the mountains of Afghanistan with Marine Infantry or back to Iraq with Marine Infantry.

...like the young sergeant from West Virginia in the Tenth Mountain Division. He was in Afghanistan when his quick reaction force was called in to protect the crash site of a U.S. helicopter that had gone down. He watched over the site while his nose was assaulted by the fumes of the wreckage—burning fuel and burning flesh. He was also on site at a weapons cache that had been discovered in Ghazni. The weapons accidentally went off, killing seven U.S. soldiers, wounding three more, and killing their Afghan interpreter. They were his brothers, men he had come to know well, played cards with, drank beer with, cussed with, talked about women with. This young man, who had lived several lifetimes within several months, reenlisted to continue his service.

...like the young lieutenant I had the privilege to meet as she became a part of the 101st Airborne Division out of Fort Campbell, Kentucky. When she arrived there, her initial assignment was to remain at Fort Campbell,

Kentucky, at the reception center while the rest of the division went forward to Iraq. She fought her way through phone calls, through pleading, through making it known that she would not stay behind as her division went forward. She fought to go to Iraq... and she went.

....like the Marine sergeant who had volunteered to go on an assault mission in Fallujah. He was one of the first Marines to enter a target house, and he took a bullet to the face. As he went down, an enemy fighter rolled a grenade into the area where he and other Marines were taking cover. As other Marines tried to make their escape, this sergeant grabbed the grenade and held it against his body taking his own life and saving the others in the room.

Countless soldiers such as these have provided aid and security in these countries, these young democracies. Back home, here in the United States, we have the safety to hear stories of our military described as automaton killing machines, or to hear a Hollywood figure ask if a U.S. Congressman would give his own child's life for the sand in Fallujah.

And I think about these soldiers and their stories. I think about the hundreds of lifetimes they've lived and what they've fought for. I ask myself is the sand of Fallujah worth their lives? Was the beach at Normandy, in World War II, worth thousands of American lives? I can tell you that the dirt in Kandahar, the desert sand in Fallujah, the beach sand in Normandy are all worthless; but the hope and freedom and security that have been bought there—by Americans, by Iraqis, by Afghans, by our allies—is priceless.

When our soldiers and our allies lay their lives on the line and pay the ultimate price, their brutal deaths are for the most noble purposes possible. They die with honor. It may be ugly, but it has depth of meaning. More meaning than drug overdoses. More meaning than deaths at the hands of gang war. More meaning than dying at the hands of a drunk driver. More meaning than being killed for no reason by a terrorist attack. All of these preventable, avoidable things have killed and will kill far more young Americans than this War on Terror ever will.

The reality is that our soldiers and our allies fight and die for a just cause, a cause that provides hope, a peace not known before in many parts of the world, a peace that is becoming known today.

Chapter 7

What the Church Says Today; What My Experience Told Me

As I grappled with this, as I saw these experiences, I came back to my early questions about peace and the morality of going to war—or of not going to war. As I looked through the lenses of a soldier, I felt compelled to look through my lenses as an ordained minister. My military experience was telling me something that today's Church in the West was not.

Midway through my tour in Afghanistan, I read the Catholic Church's 2004 World Day of Peace message that was issued as it is every year, on January 1. I read how the Church said that it was concerned that the War on Terror threatened "peaceful coexistence." But my experience told me that the enemy was not interested in coexistence. Indeed, the militant Islamists in these countries did not even want coexistence with each other. They massacred one another. I found peaceful coexistence with the Afghans on the street who worked with us. My friends deployed in Iraq found the same thing there. But the insurgents, the Taliban, these terrorists don't want peaceful coexistence, and they don't want understanding. In fact, they fear the understanding that we were gaining with the locals on the streets. Throughout history we have learned the dangers of pretending that an enemy wants coexistence when it really does not—we have only to look back seventy years to Hitler for that lesson.

The Church that year spoke of respecting international order and of the threats to that order posed by the War on Terror. But experience was telling me that this international "order" had produced and protected hundreds of tyrants and terrorists for the last thirty years, if not more. This international "order" saw the appointment of tyrants to United Nations committees for human rights. This international "order" sat idly as oppression and poverty and torture were institutionalized in many lands. This international "order" awarded a Nobel Peace Prize to Yasser Arafat, who sought to bolster this "order" in innovative ways like hijacking, suicide bombing, and early education for Palestinian four-year-olds in the doctrine of hatred for people of other cultures. This was international "order"? Where is the morality in that?

The Church spoke of upholding a commitment to peace and of the threats to that peace posed by the War on Terror. But experience forced me to ask if peace simply meant the absence of war. Because, while much of the world had been experiencing a "peace dividend" in the 1990s, other parts of the world, like Iraq and Afghanistan, weren't. Don't ask them about the threat to peace; they will ask what "peace" even means.

Indeed, the Church's own catechism (Section 2304) says

directly that peace is "not merely the absence of war," but that it is "the tranquility of order." That order is one where people can assemble freely, where people can trade freely, where people can speak freely. So what kind of a peace was the world committed to? Whose idea of peace were we committed to? In the War on Terror, I was seeing hope and freedom and real peace being extended to those who had not known it, and being protected from those who threatened and attacked it.

In that World Day of Peace message, the Church expressed concern that the War on Terror was violating basic human rights. But experience told me that basic human rights had been under siege everyday in Afghanistan and Iraq through institutionalized torture. I saw the acid scars on the women's faces in Afghanistan. I saw the videotapes of Iraqi-led torture at Abu Ghraib long before we ever got there. I saw a man's tongue being cut out in these video clips because he had dared to speak out against Saddam. I read about the institutionalized torture of women in Iraq hung upside down naked during their menstrual cycles, not to humiliate or punish them, but to humiliate their brothers or their husbands who had spoken out against Saddam. I've seen Afghans and Iraqis with an ear missing, a nose missing, fingers or hands missing because they were perceived as threats to their government because they dared to speak out. Does our peace come at the price of the basic human rights that were violated before we arrived? Did the idea of "basic human rights" apply equally to all peoples?

The Church that day spoke of the War on Terror as being punitive and repressive. But my experience on the ground was showing me that I was not a part of punitive and repressive measures, but of reconstruction, of security, of democracy and hope. Afghans were not describing this war as punitive or repressive—they were describing it as a miracle.

Finally, the Church spoke of a concern that the U.S. had developed into a culture of revenge in our response to terrorism. But my experience was telling me that ours is a culture of hope, freedom, tolerance, respect and security. We do not seek to occupy; we seek to rid the world of tyranny. We have only to look at our World War II enemies in Japan and Western Europe to see that ours has not been a drive to occupy. On the contrary, we helped to rebuild these once-vanquished enemies to levels where they can challenge us today, politically and economically. We have provided assistance to Muslims after tsunamis in Indonesia and after earthquakes in Iran—apparently the "Great Satan" does have a good heart. We were the Christian nation that protected Muslim Bosnians from Christian Serbs. We were the "occupiers" who have helped pave (and then get out of) the way for self-government, evidenced by the purple fingers held aloft in Afghanistan and Iraq.

This is a culture of revenge? I submit that we have been a culture of responsibility and service, a culture of hope.

The Church had been telling me one thing, but my experiences were telling me something very different—and it was confirming my conscience. And so I sought to ensure that both my conscience and my experience were properly aligned. My search took me to the history of the Church.

Chapter 8

WHAT THE CHURCH IN HISTORY HAS SAID

I looked beyond what the Church had been telling me in recent years, and, indeed, what the Church had been telling me about war in general for the last thirty or forty years. I looked to the Scriptures and read about the value of laying down one's life for a friend. (You can't lay down your life for a friend if you do not engage what threatens that friend.)

I read the Sermon on the Mount, specifically the message, "Blessed are the peacemakers." I read about how war will occur on earth as good triumphs over evil. I read about Christ's anger in the Temple as he drove people out. What I've read in the New Testament can be found in the Old Testament.

I read the words of the Apostle Paul describing the soldier as one who bears the sword not in vain, but as a protector of others from those who do evil. I read the exhortation of the Psalmist to deliver the needy out of the hands of sinners— no easy task spiritually or physically.

I looked to the centuries of Judeo-Christian tradition built upon natural law, which has been the foundation for all human law. Natural law sets forth that people live in organized societies and that these societies, in turn, require authority. That authority must have a moral foundation to control its members who may stray and to direct the common good. Our tradition recognizes that societies have a right to protect themselves and a right to assert themselves when moral authority is absent or, worse, negligent. It's called the right of war.

The Catholic encyclopedia tells us that we have this natural right of war and that we may execute it in three ways: defensively if we are attacked; offensively if we are threatened (a "preemptive strike," to use today's terms); punitively if we have seen one party exercise extreme brutality against another. Like all natural rights, the right of war can be—and has been—abused. But also like all natural rights, it cannot be disputed. From the encyclopedia itself:

> *Catholic philosophy, therefore, concedes to the State the full natural right of war, whether defensive, as in case of another's attack in force upon it; offensive (more properly, coercive), where it finds it necessary to take the initiative in the application of force; or punitive, in the infliction of punishment for evil done against itself or, in some determined cases, against others. International law views the punitive right of war with suspicion; but, though it is open to wide abuse, its original existence under the natural law cannot well be disputed... In English this term [natural law] is frequently employed as equivalent to the laws of nature, meaning the order which governs the activities of the material universe. Among the Roman jurists natural law designated those*

instincts and emotions common to man and the lower animals, such as the instinct of self-preservation and love of offspring. In its strictly ethical application–the sense in which this article treats it–the natural law is the rule of conduct which is prescribed to us by the Creator in the constitution of the nature with which He has endowed us.

I read Augustine, who said, "True religion looks upon as peaceful those wars that are waged not for motives of aggrandizement, or cruelty, but with the object of securing peace, of punishing evil-doers, and of uplifting the good… We do not seek peace in order to be at war, but we go to war that we may have peace."

I read Thomas Aquinas, who a thousand years ago, spoke of war not in terms of "War" or "Justice," but in terms of "Charity." He claimed that war could be an act of love, recognizing that there can be a peace that is so brutal, a peace that is so corrupt that it takes an act of war to restore human dignity and respect as a last resort, and that war is necessary to destroy an unjust peace. In this context the Protestant leader Calvin described the soldier as an agent of God's love.

Aquinas and others have spoken of "Just War". And there are four common conditions that have existed through the centuries for Just War.

The first condition of just war is that *the damage by the aggressor must be lasting, grave and certain.* As I looked at my experience I examined this condition. I thought about Bin Laden's call in 1998 for the death of all Americans and Jews. He's not hiding his intentions; it is clear that his actions have been lasting, grave and certain. As Al-Qaeda was chased out of Afghanistan, it fled to Iraq, which was becoming the next Afghanistan, the next sanctuary, training field, and planning place for the next attack against the U.S. on U.S. soil.

Saddam's torture in Iraq was lasting, grave and certain for decades. Without doubt he had used the weapons of mass destruction (that we knew he had) against the Kurds, his domestic enemies, and against the Iranians, his foreign enemies. When he had it he used it—it was lasting, grave and certain.

When I thought about the second condition of Just War—*that other means are found to be ineffective*—I thought about the twelve-year embargo on Iraq that followed the Gulf War. I thought about the "effectiveness" of this embargo, as I recalled the forty luxurious palaces that Saddam built after the Gulf War and during the embargo. I thought about the two hundred Western companies that did business under the table in direct violation of the embargo, enriching Saddam and enriching themselves with his blood money. I thought about how this embargo was only getting weaker, only becoming more of a joke, by the year as Saddam bided his time.

I thought about the results announced by the Iraqi Survey Group: that within a week of giving the thumbs up, Saddam could produce anthrax; that within three months of giving the thumbs up, he would be back in the business of producing chemical weapons, as he was already purchasing precursor agents. I thought about when, in 1998, the United Nations weapons inspectors had been forced out of Iraq, that Saddam had raised the salaries of his nuclear scientists ten times, giving them the signal that their skills were needed and that they would be brought to bear and used again. In 1997, Iraq only had forty "military technical research" projects in development; that number of projects exploded to 3,200 over the four years that would follow the departure of UN weapons inspectors. If, indeed, Saddam no longer had weapons of mass destruction in 2003, he certainly was more than ready to develop and deploy them as a result of having maintained—and expanded—his capabilities. In a particularly evil twist, he was prepared, in the event the embargo was lifted, to use the riches he'd made from the Oil For Food programs to restore his WMD capability. He had proven that he would use it because he used it in the past.

And how "effective" had we been with our means of addressing the problems in Afghanistan? Quite simply, we abandoned them after the Soviets pulled out, allowing the likes of the Taliban to come to power. We knew Al-Qaeda and Bin Laden were operating there. As he continued to attack us throughout the 1990s, we'd lob a cruise missile and offer ultimatums. This method of diplomacy so "deterred" Bin Laden that he decided to fly two airplanes into the World Trade Center, one into the Pentagon and had another one destined for Washington. Indeed, our response had been ineffective.

I thought about the third condition of just war, *the likelihood of success,* as I heard many people concerned that the efforts in Afghanistan and Iraq were not showing any success. But then I thought about the full picture of what I was seeing on the ground: reconstruction was happening, even as we fought; elections were happening, even as we fought. I put this in historical perspective, looking back upon events such as World War II, with its six years of intense combat, followed by ten years of reconstruction and full military occupation with a million men on the ground in both Germany and Japan.

Yet I look at the War on Terror. We have accomplished far more in the first five years of this active war than we did during the first five years of occupation in World War II—after the six years of intense combat. We lost millions of people in World War II; we have lost a few thousand soldiers in the War on Terror. Each of these sacrifices is sacred, but they are dwarfed in number by the casualties of the War of Independence, the Civil War, World War I, and World War II—all of them deemed successes by history.

Consider these successes in five years of the War on Terror:

- No terror attack on United States soil since September 11, 2001;
- Constitutions written and approved in both Afghanistan and Iraq;
- Multiple elections with full suffrage in both Afghanistan and Iraq
- Voter turnout in Afghanistan and Iraq that far outdraws that of the United States;
- Afghanistan is now the only fully functioning democracy in Central Asia and Iraq is the only one in the Middle East outside of Israel;
- Muammar Qaddafi's weapons of mass destruction are now in the United States; diplomatic relations have been restored with Libya;
- Democratic elections—many in their infancies—are being held in Arab countries where they've never been held before... and with the participation of women;
- Banking systems re-established in Afghanistan and Iraq;
- Fewer than 3,000 combat deaths in the War on Terror during five years of war—a miraculous number compared to previous wars;
- Torture as an institutional norm eradicated from Afghanistan and Iraq;
- Immense reconstruction—with much left to do— even while combat continues; in past wars reconstruction only began after complete destruction.

Indeed, the likelihood of success comes down to commitment. The military has a strategic term called Center of Gravity. It is that point where a society's war-making capability collapses, resulting in the total collapse of whatever goals the initiative set out to achieve. The Center of Gravity is like the hub of the wheel: you can lose a few spokes, but the wheel can keep turning. But when that hub is gone, all the spokes fall, and the wheel collapses.

In a democracy, and especially in the United States, that Center of Gravity is the public will. And that is what our enemy is attacking. The enemy knows that a roadside bomb's target is not simply the U.S. soldiers it will maim or kill; it is primarily the public will of the American people. While the explosive does not render us ineffective in the tactical arena, it can render us ineffective in the public arena. That is why the enemy attacks the way it does. That is why they target aid workers, contract workers, local civilians. This goes right to the gut of our will.

Success is not easy; it comes with time, commitment and perseverance.

The fourth condition of just war is *proportionality*. Put simply, it means don't overdo it; you don't need a cinder block to kill a fly. I think about proportionality as we fight this war. I think about the billions of dollars we have been invested in precision bombs. Walking through the streets in Kabul, I marvel when I see a building completely reduced to rubble while the rest of the buildings that surround it remain standing. Precision bombs can do this quite effectively, though not always perfectly. Sure, the damage may extend beyond the targeted building, or the wrong building may be struck, but there are no cities in Afghanistan or Iraq that look like Dresden. It is far more expensive to use precision weapons than it is to firebomb.

We have invested billions of dollars in precision weaponry. It is a reflection of the value we have on innocent life, to reduce "collateral" and unnecessary damage. We spare no expense when it comes to sparing innocent lives.

The basic weapon of the infantryman is a reflection of proportionality and our value of life. Look at the weapon of choice for the enemy—the AK-47. It is durable and it is cheap to make. It is easy to maintain. You can drag it through mud. You can bang it against a tree. You can ignore it for days on end as sand covers it. And yet you can pick it back up and squeeze the trigger and fire a shot. You may not hit your target with one bullet (accuracy is not the norm), but that doesn't matter, because you can spray your target, and everything else in the vicinity, with bullets.

Now look at the basic tool of the infantryman of the United States—the M16. It is very sensitive and very expensive. Any soldier who has spent more than a couple of hours with one will tell you that when it gets a little bit of sand or dirt in it, it will jam up on you. You put your own life at risk carrying one in combat. A soldier will tell you that if you're not shooting the M16, you'd better be cleaning the M16, so it will be ready when you need it. But the M16 has few peers for accuracy. I can point my M16 at a crowd of people 500 yards away, and I can take out one enemy target and leave everyone else standing.

The AK-47 and the M16: their differences tell us something about proportionality.

I reflected upon these four conditions of just war, and I reflected upon the Scriptures, and I reflected upon my own experiences—and the image that came to my mind was that of two shepherds: David and Jesus. The image itself was the idealized, sanitized Western image of shepherds: men who are lily-white, silk-skinned, who look loving and peaceful, as they hold and cuddle a lamb, the picture of innocence and love.

And then I think about the shepherds that I've seen, the real ones, in Afghanistan. Shepherds in Afghanistan are much the same as shepherds two thousand years ago—except for the occasional cell phone antenna sticking up from their ears. They are coarse. They are tough. They are brutish. They are dirty. They have blood on them, because they have to protect their sheep. They have to engage wolves with their own hands to protect their sheep.

That is the image that the early Christians had of Jesus, and that the Jews had of David. They invoked the image of shepherds for a reason, not because shepherds were soft and cuddly, but because Jesus and David were tough and willing to engage the enemy, to protect people from evil, whether physical or spiritual. That is what a shepherd does.

Chapter 9

WHY WE MUST WIN THIS WAR

These images, thoughts and prayers brought me back to my initial challenge and my questions: What is peace? What is the morality of going to war? What is the morality of not going to war? And I asked myself, what is our threshold of brutality? How many sheep do we sacrifice? I was caught again in the crossfire of contradictory questions.

I realize we have obligations and responsibilities. That God has given us minds to think and eyes to see. Yes, we all want things to be nice. Yes, we want things to be full of joy and peace. That is what we strive for. But it is dangerous for us to confuse idealism with fantasy. We have to face the ugly truth of this world. And the truth of this world is that evil exists.

Hitler was real. That was truth, and it was ugly. As I saw the after effects of his reign when, in the 1980s, I visited the concentration camp in Dachau, I saw ugliness. Stalin was real. That was truth, and it was ugly. As I spoke to the survivors of the purges and the gulags in Russia, as I met the families from the gulags, as I saw the environmental and economic damage to Eastern Europe, I saw ugliness. And in my own homeland, slavery in the South was real. That was truth, and it was ugly—and its damage is lasting. I have seen evil and brutality in all of these places... And I've seen it in Afghanistan and Iraq.

From the fires of evil, however, I have seen the light of hope. And it is showing the way to peace. I have seen it in a free Germany, far from the Germany of Dachau, where millions of Muslims flock in order to find jobs and freedom. I have seen it in Russia and Eastern Europe, with markets flourishing, economies taking off, people speaking and voting without fear of punishment. I have seen it in the South, the birthplace of America's civil rights movement, where so much good has happened (and still much more is needed)... And I've seen it in Afghanistan and Iraq.

I have seen hope in the face of the safe house manager who told me of the miracle of the two years following our entry into Kabul. I have seen it in the face of the orphan girl who told me she wanted to be a doctor, and the one who said, "I will be president." I have seen it in the face of that young lady from Farah Province in Afghanistan, now serving as an elected Parliamentarian. I have seen it in the refugees returning to Afghanistan and in the Iraqis holding steadfast in their towns and villages. I have seen it in the Iraqi recruits who get back in line after bombs have taken their friends, their cousins and their brothers. I have seen it on the purple fingers of men—and women—in Afghanistan and Iraq.

I have seen it in the uniforms worn by soldiers I have known and served with. The Afghans I have served have seen that hope in my uniform. (They have not seen that hope in my minister's robe.)

I have seen it in my own children at home in America. I see hope. I know hope.

My wife has explained it in a way far better than I ever could. When I returned home from Afghanistan, I was out one day when a repairman came by our house. He saw my military gear still strewn about. My wife told him I had just returned from Afghanistan. The young man said to my wife, "You know, I served in the 101st in the nineties. I got out long before 9-11, but I know guys that are over there, although I'm not in touch with them anymore. I see what's on the news. And I wonder, is this right? I'm just not sure what to think about this war. But your husband's been there. What does he think?"

And she said to him, "Well, before my husband went to Afghanistan he thought it was right. But now that he's been there and now that he's home, he knows it's right."

I can say with full confidence that I know our cause in the War on Terror is just and that it is necessary. I have found resolution. I know this war is moral. I know this War on Terror is an act of love and justice for those we protect at home, for those we liberate abroad, and yes, in some incomprehensible way, to those who challenge us. Our enemies and our soldiers in the field today are determining our future. Everyday we at home also have to decide what we are going to do about this war.

We are all called to serve one another, in some way. It is the true meaning of vocation. I have been called to serve in two ways: militarily and pastorally. Some may view these two distinct calls as incompatible or contradictory. I view them as distinctly separate but equal. I believe vocations are calls to service, and that we are called to serve in different—and, for some of us, many ways. I believe that when serving the common good in an authentic, just way there can be no contradiction.

What I believe is contradictory is the Christian who ignored slavery. What I believe is contradictory is the Christian who ignored Nazism. What I believe is contradictory, indeed, is the Christian who not only failed to recognize Communism for what it was but who even dared to support it. Well, terrorism is the greatest threat that this country has ever faced. And I am one Christian who will not ignore it.

Withdrawal is not an option. In fact, withdrawal is an illusion because this fight is on and this fight has been on long before that fateful Tuesday morning in 2001. We will either fight there or we will fight here, as we found out on September 11. This war is a long war, and all that we believe in is at stake. We cannot withdraw from a war that is being waged upon us—it's our war as much as it is Afghanistan's or Iraq's. Our only options now are victory or defeat.

Our country needs soldiers. Our soldiers and our government need active support. And so we all have to ask ourselves everyday, what am I going to do about the future? What am I going to do to serve others? How am I going to serve? If we love our values, if we value freedom, if we seek authentic peace for others and security for future generations, if we are to wage true love in this world, then we must continue to wage this War on Terror. If there is to be a time of true peace then now must be a time for war— a war that is a last resort for a time for love.

Chapter 10

Q & A:
COMMON QUESTIONS,
UNCOMMON ANSWERS

As I was being encouraged by many people to write a book about my war experiences in the context of my ministry and faith, many recommended that I use a question and answer format so readers could be better prepared to talk about the necessity of this war. While I hope that there are many valuable points covered in the narrative that describes how I came to answer many of my own questions, I have decided to use the question and answer format here for those questions that I am most often asked on my lecture tours.

The following are questions that reflect the ones most commonly asked that would not naturally be part of my own story. My story addresses my own questions regarding faith and war, and to those I can speak with direct knowledge. The following questions are those for which I do not have firsthand knowledge, but to which I can but offer an opinion based on my experiences.

WHERE IS OSAMA BIN LADEN MOST LIKELY LOCATED? WHY HAVEN'T WE FOUND HIM?

At my level of service, I had no direct or even indirect exposure that would allow me to answer either of these questions authoritatively and factually. However, I can provide some opinions and observations formed from more experience and analysis than most have had the opportunity to have.

According to the most common analysis, Bin Laden most likely is somewhere between Afghanistan and Pakistan. I agree with that. Former CIA Director Porter Goss at one time stated he had an "excellent idea" of Bin Laden's location and we have to suspect he was speaking from a foundation of knowledge, not just a good hunch.

We have to remember that if Bin Laden is in the Afghan/Pakistan mountains he is in some of the most inhospitable terrain in the world—which means it is very hospitable for someone trying to hide. Remember also that it took 20 years to find Ted Kaczynski, the Unabomber, hiding in the Rockies—and he was found only after authorities received a tip from his brother. Remember again that it took years to find Eric Rudolph, the abortion clinic bomber, who was hiding in the Smokies. And he was found not in the mountains, but in a restaurant dumpster in North Georgia, where he was rummaging.

Bin Laden is likely located in terrain much rougher than the Rockies and the Smokies. (It is unlikely he will be rummaging through a dumpster at a fast food restaurant in Jalalabad any time soon.) Plus, unlike Kaczynski and Rudolph, he has an entire network of people devoted to protecting and supporting him. So the odds do not favor us.

Another important point to consider is that we may be much better off simply knowing generally where he is and leaving it at that. Al-Qaeda is the real target; neutralizing it is most important. A dead—martyred—Bin Laden could be a rallying cry for his supporters, causing much more trouble for us. Bin Laden in captivity could turn out to be very problematic, becoming the three-ring circus we have seen with Saddam Hussein and others. It could be that we have him right where we want him and right where we need him, cut off and neutralized. (Or should we say neutered?)

SINCE YOU [THE AUTHOR] HAVE TAKEN THE GOVERNMENT POSITION HOOK, LINE AND SINKER ABOUT THE WAR, DO YOU THINK WE'VE MADE ANY MISTAKES?

Yes. You bet we have made mistakes. And mistakes are made in every war and always will be. That does not mean that the cause is wrong and should be abandoned—far from it. In fact, it means it is all the more important to correct those mistakes so that we do not put our cause at further risk.

From my humble, small role in the war, I believe we have made three miscalculations and that we had two things go the wrong way for us.

First, the three miscalculations:

> 1. We should have increased our military dramatically following 9-11. Too often in modern history a dramatic drawdown in our regular forces causes us to be unprepared for the next "real world" threat that comes our way. It happened following World War I. Had we a larger military in the 1930s we may have been able to deter the rise of Hitler to a significant degree, or at the least been able to respond faster and more effectively. (In the years it took to build back our capacities, many Europeans died and the Holocaust grew ever greater in scope). A large military build-up is likely what saved us from a catastrophic confrontation with the Soviets. A large military is one of the most moral actions we can take, because it deters aggression in the first place.

While it is true that large conventional armies are not designed for terrorist/insurgent-based threats such as Al-Qaeda, they can deter states from sponsoring terrorism. There is a role for large numbers of troops in the post-direct-combat phase of the kind of war we are now fighting. If we had a larger military in reserve and at the ready, Iran may not be acting as boldly and belligerently as it is—and, of course, our military would not be as stretched as it is. All of our debate about our military readiness is only helping the enemy.

After 9-11 we had a huge window of opportunity for aggressive recruiting. I still think an aggressive recruiting drive featuring celebrities of all types (political, athletic, entertainment, business, etc.) and an appeal to what is most important—freedom and a civil world—would lead to a rise in forces. The key to the readiness debate is having a military large enough to never raise the question of readiness, either in our minds or, more important, in the minds of our enemies. Their perception is the perception that counts when it comes to deterrence. And that will save lives, preserve security and offer hope.

2. After 9-11, the administration urged Americans to live their lives as normal. I understand where it was coming from, but I believe it was a bad call. Yes, we did not want the terrorists to think they had scored some sort of victory by changing our way of life. But it is quite clear that war is not a normal way of life (and it shouldn't be); it demands that we change our lives. We are at war, and yet people are beginning to forget that we are in a real war precisely because they are living their lives "like normal." If it were not for the involvement of the National Guard and

Reserve, most communities might forget all together that we are in a war. And when people lose touch they lose the sense of purpose. Instead, the administration should have identified some reasonable and meaningful venues of shared sacrifice that would pull the nation together. My parents went through rationing and curbs on liberty of the most dramatic forms during WWII. They even had blackouts at night in Louisville—even though the chances of a Luftwaffe attack in Kentucky were rather small. But even by saving electricity they were doing something together.

3. We absolutely did need more troops in the post-combat phase of the Iraq campaign, and more in Afghanistan as well. The amount of combat power needed to bring down the Hussein and Taliban regimes was spot on, but the number of troops needed to restore security in both places has been short. Remember that it took a million soldiers each in Japan and Germany—for ten years—to rebuild. We are currently rebuilding even as we fight.

We saw in Afghanistan during my tour of service the difference it makes when you can leave units in a single place for an extended time. It is dramatic. It is all about building trust and relationships, which is particularly critical in the Middle East and Central Asian cultures. When we come through for a week and don't return for another month or more, the locals have no reason to assist us—their lives are on the line for cooperating. And we have no mechanism in that case for ensuring they are properly using aid, instead of hoarding it or selling it.

When Lieutenant General David Barno, the commander in Afghanistan at the time, adopted the approach of extended stays in single places, we suddenly went from hearing a majority of that region's reports addressing rocket attacks and IEDs to a majority of that region's reports addressing weapons cache turn-ins, increased intelligence reporting, and more effective use—and results—of aid funds. The problem was that we didn't have enough troops to do this in more places. It takes lots of boots on ground in lots of places to build trust and accountability. It's as simple as that. General Shinseki may have been wrong about berets, but he was right where it mattered about troop-to-task numbers in today's war.

And now for two critical areas that went the wrong way for us:

1. We failed to establish a northern front from Turkey for the campaign into Iraq. This hurt us much more than we realized it would. Had we been able to attack with at least an Army Division from the north, we would have been able to cut off escape routes into the Sunni Triangle for the Iraqi military. Instead of disappearing into society, these forces would have been attacked or captured. The northern and southern hammers would have slammed these enemy forces together with little chance for escape. As it happened, the Iraqi military was able to disperse and matriculate north. We were also unable to cut off escape routes into Syria fast enough as a result.

2. The Spanish withdrawal from Iraq following the Madrid subway bombing marked the beginning of a major sea shift in momentum in the campaign. Let's examine the six months prior to this withdrawal from Iraq in April 2004. Coalition forces had survived their first Ramadan in Iraq in better-than-expected fashion

in November 2003 (Ramadan is a religious season in the Fall which is usually very tense due to heightened Islamic religious fervor). The following month, we captured Saddam Hussein. The huge success of the Afghan Loya Jirga in approving a constitution within the same month added to U.S. momentum in the war. Then, in early winter, Muammar Qaddafi of Libya announced he was basically switching sides to the U.S. and sending his weapons of mass destruction to Oak Ridge, Tennessee. This was a major victory in the war, as Qaddafi had sensed the momentum in the war was dramatically going our way. If he had waited a couple of months, he may have made a different assessment. The public portrayal of events at Abu Ghraib, the protracted defense of Fallujah that April, and the Spanish withdrawal all culminated in a 180-degree shift in our momentum. It was exactly what Al-Qaeda needed, and they got it—a major confidence builder for them. The Spanish withdrawal had minimal impact from a tactical and troop strength standpoint, but the message it sent to the enemy (complete capitulation) and to the allies (count us out), resulted in a severe strategic impact which greatly contributed to a shift in the course of the war.

What about the proposed U.S. ports deal with the United Arab Emirates? How could the Bush Administration have considered turning our security over to "them"?

I'm no political expert so I'm sure the issue could have been handled better from all sorts of standpoints. Objectively (and rationally) speaking, this was not a bad deal. More important, the way it ended is likely to hurt us strategically. I found it interesting that the average union-member longshoreman I heard in multiple interviews couldn't understand what all the fuss was about. Our people would continue doing the work and providing the security. In previous conflicts we've had stranger bedfellows, including the Soviet Union during World War II. The UAE, along with other Persian Gulf states, had made a dramatic turnaround in their foreign policy (much like Qaddafi in Libya) by placing their bets—and their strategic interests—with us. If we are going to win the War on Terror, we will have to cooperate with Arab governments at the highest levels. The ports deal wasn't even really at this level in terms of our own risk exposure. But the message it sent to our Arab allies and particularly to the Arab masses via al-Jazeera was, "We don't trust you at all. You are all terrorists." So much for the "reaching out and building understanding" that is so often talked about as a preferred strategy by those opposed to the war.

WHAT ABOUT THE PUBLIC CRITICISM BY SEVERAL GENERALS OF SECRETARY RUMSFELD?

I may be a lowly Major in the National Guard, but I am one of those people that our Generals are supposed to be leading and inspiring. I just have a question of my own: at which point were they showing the least amount of leadership—was it when they kept quiet and followed a war plan that they supposedly knew was all wrong and would get our soldiers unnecessarily killed, or is it now when they are covering their backs in order to protect their reputations in history? It seems to me that they have now ensured their reputations in history. Disagreements over tactics and strategy are legitimate and necessary. But making those discussions available as tools of propaganda by the enemy is not the responsible forum for those discussions.

We have needed a strong and resolute Secretary of Defense. And we have one.

Yes, it's too bad that oppression exists in other lands. But we wouldn't want others coming over to fix us.

I'm from Tennessee. Just over 150 years ago or so we used to oppress people under the then-legal institution of slavery. It took people coming from outside our region to set us straight. And there is still resentment and arguments over that war and about the alternatives to solving that problem. But I, for one, am glad that that institution has been thrown into the dust bin of history where it belongs. We still have progress to make, but it took "outsiders" to get us started.

What is the impact of critical comments on the war effort by the likes of Senator Durbin, Representative Murtha and Al Gore when they claim we are torturing and rounding up Arabs and losing the war?

It is huge and it doesn't help us. They are feeding the enemy's propaganda machine in ways that even the enemy cannot fathom. It suggests to the enemy that the U.S. lacks the will to win, and that it cannot stick it out through any tough long-term conflict to victory. Their comments weaken our own center of gravity.

We never have and likely never will lose tactically in a conflict. We lose at strategic levels, and this war is primarily a strategic war being fought in the information arena. Al-Qaeda attacks us through the media, and strikes fear in the hearts of those who would fight with us through the media. We shouldn't be giving them the ammunition. That is how we will lose this war, if it comes to that. There is certainly a place for politicians to debate and disagree but it is not in Al-Jazeera.

What about the National Security Agency wiretapping American phone calls?

The American public seems to sense the necessity of monitoring phone calls to and from terrorists, especially at the general level. The vast majority of us have nothing to worry about. This goes back to my assertion earlier that we need to make sacrifices in times of war; we've done it before and we should be doing it now. In my personal experience, not one letter I sent home had been opened and had lines marked out on it by censors. My family in WWII received letters marked up like that from my great uncles when they served and every single call from Europe to the states was listened to by monitors. In my case letters flowed freely as did email and phone calls. If they were monitored, my privacy was not affected in any other way.

Most people probably agree with you about Afghanistan, but what about Iraq? Isn't it based on a lie, and hasn't it actually hurt our efforts in Afghanistan?

Afghanistan and Iraq are not separate wars. They are interrelated and actually two campaigns in the same war, probably even more interrelated than the Germany and Japan campaigns during World War II.

The war in Iraq is not based on a lie. At the time we went to war, everyone thought Saddam Hussein had weapons of mass destruction. As I outline in my book he maintained, at the very least, a level of capacity for WMD that made the threat a credible and imminent one. To have let a weak embargo get even weaker and a strong Saddam get even stronger would have been completely irresponsible, especially given his history and his emerging relationship with Al-Qaeda. In fact the issue isn't whether we acted too soon against Saddam in March 2003, the issue is why we waited so long. Time was Saddam's friend and we gave him plenty of it.

The campaign in Iraq has not distracted us from Afghanistan. In fact, it has aided our overall efforts in the War on Terror and probably even in Afghanistan. We know in the wake of the fall of the Taliban that Al-Qaeda operatives were fleeing to Iraq. It was fast becoming the next terrorist sanctuary from which the next attacks against the U.S. were being planned. Fighting terrorist insurgents in Iraq is much more preferable to fighting a larger force in Afghanistan. The terrain is more favorable and the strategic location is much more favorable. Making Iraq the magnet for terrorist fighters gave us a much more advantageous battlefield than Afghanistan—and it's certainly far better than doing so on our own soil. If we were not fighting in Iraq, our efforts would likely be worse off in Afghanistan (which saw far less Al-Qaeda activity in light of its new focus on Iraq) and we would quite possibly be fighting terrorist cells in Europe and the U.S. instead.

Don't atrocities such as those at Abu Ghraib, Haditha, Fallujah, and Hamindiyah illustrate the unjustness of this war and why we should just end it?

The reality of war is ugly. Bad things happen. Mistakes are made. When a cameraman filmed a Marine shooting a terrorist in Fallujah who allegedly was wounded and allegedly posed no threat, he captured the essence of the ugly split-second of war. This is where reality gets ugly, when the wrong split-second decision will cost one life or the other—or many. The Marine who had to make that split-second decision with the indicators he had (previous enemy contact and a recent similar situation) made the only decision he could make—and he could not hesitate. It may look one way to a guy who carries a camera. I can assure you that it looks different to a guy carrying a gun and the weight of responsibility for the lives of those in the room with him—including the cameraman.

Watch the movie, *Saving Private Ryan,* and count how many war crimes you see. (There's plenty.) That movie is a brilliant display of both the inhumanity and the humanity of war. Unfortunately, war consists of both. But the crimes that may take place—and which should be punished thoroughly—do not detract from the validity and the justice of the cause. Had we pulled out of World War II because a photojournalist had recorded someone like the sergeant in *Saving Private Ryan* who shot POWs after giving them some smokes, Hitler would have continued his mass atrocities.

Where these crimes have occurred, they must be punished. But they must not be presented in such a way that they cause a distraction from pursuing the victory that is vital. They must not be presented in such a way that our enemy can use these isolated incidents against us. When a police officer shoots the wrong man in a hot pursuit we do not withdraw our police force. We are different from our enemy; we are deeply offended by acts of deliberate violence against civilians or true torture of captives. This is also why we must win.

Isn't it all just about oil in the end?

Some say the war is over oil. That's always a good distraction. I do think perhaps there is some merit to that argument, but not for the typical reasons given. Afghanistan has no oil. (Perhaps that's why we ignored that country once the Soviets left.) Of course if there had been oil there, we never would have let the Soviets invade—or perhaps they would have been there already, long before the last decades of the 20th century when these conflicts came to a head. Perhaps that lack of oil caused us to ignore Afghanistan to the extent that a regime like the Taliban could rise, thereby allowing that country to become a terrorist sanctuary for Al-Qaeda, thereby leading to the greatest external attack on U.S. soil in our history.

The Middle East is full of oil. Perhaps that's why we've treated the region with kid gloves for so long, tolerating the most brutal of dictators for "regional stability" and for peace at any price. It seems to me those days are gone in steering our foreign policy. And, quite frankly, I'm proud to be part of that change. And even if it is for oil to some extent, I'm in no hurry to go back to the pre-oil society. Like it or not, oil is, at this moment in time, the lifeblood of our economy, our security, and our freedom. Those are things worth dying and fighting for.

Acknowledgements

There are so many people to whom I am so grateful to for their support, encouragement and tangible contributions to this work. There are so many who made this possible either indirectly, directly or both.

In addition to those to whom this work is dedicated I want to publicly thank the following.

To those who inspired and encouraged me: Fr Pat Kibby - pastor of the Cathedral and friend; Susan Austin-Crumpton who has always played a key role in the turning points of my adult life. Thank you both! Major General Gus Hargett, the Adjutant General of the Tennessee National Guard - MG Hargett has made it his mission to put respect into the term "weekend warrior" as he welcomes home every single Tennessee Guardsman who returns from war to Tennessee. I used to detest the term as one of derision. Our General tells us a story when we return of how the "weekend warrior" epitomizes everything that is beautiful about the American spirit - those who prepare and are ready to leave everything behind at a moment's notice to secure those at home and to bring hope to others abroad. Thank you, Sir. I am proud to be one of your weekend warriors. Lieutenant Colonel Paul W. Rainwater - close friend since Officer Basic Course and who is the model of Christian public service including two tours in the War on Terror. Major Chris Beaver, we've grown up together as young officers into field grade officers in the Guard and are more like brothers than friends.

Others include Colonel Harold "Red" Roberts, Colonel Jewell Fields, Colonel Russ Thaden, Colonel Eddy Daley, Captain Kevin Frank (USN), Colonel Tom Snukis, Colonel Michael Boardman, Lieutenant Colonel Cheryl Lanke (USAF), Major Robert Zickgraf, Captain Pam Elliott, Chief Warrant Officer Rick Thorne, Sergeant First Class Ronald Cannon, Staff Sergeant Russell Parman, Sergeant Matthew Effinger, and Jeff Moore.

Also, Reverend Mister Mark Faulkner, Ray Van Hooser, Homer Van Hooser, Joan Ussery, Amanda Taylor and Mary Maynard. Last but not at all least, Reverend Mister Jim McKenzie, Lois Jones, Lori Reddick, Darlene Reilly, Suzanne Southworth, Mary Corby, Lisa Vegors and "Mustard" Chandler.

To those who not only inspired but made a tangible contribution to this work: Lieutenant Colonel Patty Jones (friend and mentor), Lieutenant Colonel Eddie Farmer, Lieutenant Colonel Tony and Michelle Morales (the best friends the Krensons could ever have!!), Bruce Barbour, Tom Murphy, Julie O'Connor, Jeff Spodnik, William V. Blazek, Jr. S.J. (who's been in my shoes in so many ways), Patrick McGuffy (whose military and spiritual advice before deployment and since has been critical), Lee and Diane

Carter (to both of whom I am grateful for so many reasons) and the folks at Young America's Foundation - Ron Robinson, Patrick Coyle, Andrew Coffin, Flagg Youngblood, Roger Custer - who have given me a wonderful platform to continue my mission.

Finally to the people who made this happen - the "doers", those who shared the vision and did the hard work: Steve Brallier (guide and friend in my new world), my editor Ken Anselment (if it read well it's to his credit; if it didn't - well he can't help what he had to work with - you should have seen it before he got it :), Patsy Hibbett (my aunt and transcriber), Charlie Flood (friend, partner, publisher and especially inspiration), Gary Bozeman (designer), Johnny Shea and Cameron, Mark, and Avery Dipasquale for the use of the baptism photo on the front cover. Lynn Williams (publicist and credibility check), Suzie Schulenberg (web site design), and especially Reverend Donald Sensing - role model in all respects of friend, minister, soldier, husband, father, writer, citizen, servant.

Thank you all.

jgk

Nashville, TN
June 2006

SPEAKING ENGAGEMENTS

John Krenson has spoken to a variety of business, civic, church and college groups regarding his reconciliation between faith and war, between calls of service to the ministry and the military.

These include: Bucknell University, Franciscan University at Steubenville Ohio, University of Baltimore, University of Michigan at Ann Arbor, Marquette University, Mary Washington University, Warren County Community College of New Jersey, Belhaven College, Chamberlain Hunt Military Academy, State University of New York at Brockport, various Rotary Clubs, Exchange Clubs, Sertoma Clubs, high schools, book clubs, and other business clubs. Deacon Krenson also leads retreats and classes around the issue of Just War theology and its practical application in American history.

For booking a lecture at college campuses please contact Mr. Pat Coyle at Young America's Foundation **800-USA-1776**.

For more information to schedule other events please visit **www.johnkrenson.com**.

Printed in the United States
84661LV00006B/67/A